Jeni114

CAMEL DRIVERS ARE OVER THE HUMP

DRACULA WAS BATTY

HEIDI HAS A
SWISS BANK ACCOUNT

OLIVER
IS A
LITTLE DICKENS

MAID MARION MARRIED A HOOD

KING ARTHUR
RUNS A
KNIGHT SCHOOL

OLD KING COLE
HAD SOUL

COWBOYS HAVE CHAPPED KNEES

THE ST. LAWRENCE RIVER
IS HEADED FOR A FALL

MADAME BUTTERFLY WAS
ONCE A CATERPILLAR

MAGIC CARPETS HAVE TURBAN ENGINES

JOAN OF ARC WAS A FRENCH FRY

TAXIDERMISTS ARE STUFFY PEOPLE

PETER PAN WAS A FLY BY NIGHT

STAPLES GET IT ALL TOGETHER

DRACULA EATS AND RUNS

CENTAURS LIKE TO HORSE AROUND

LITTLE BO PEEP RUNS AROUND WITH A CROOK

THE RIO GRANDE TAKES IN BORDERS

PUNS, GAGS, QUIPS AND RIDDLES

A Collection of Dreadful Jokes

Roy Doty

DOUBLEDAY & COMPANY, INC.
GARDEN CITY, NEW YORK

ISBN: 0-385-06051-3 Trade
       0-385-06057-2 Prebound
Library of Congress Catalog Card Number 73-13116
Copyright © 1974 by Roy Doty
All Rights Reserved
Printed in the United States of America
9 8 7 6 5 4 3 2

7060

ROY DOTY is a nationally known free-lance artist whose work regularly appears in numerous major publications, such as *Newsweek*, *Business Week* and the *New York Times*. He is familiar to *Popular Science* readers as author-cartoonist of the monthly "Wordless Workshop," and his "Laugh-In" newspaper comic strip is nationally syndicated. He is presently at work illustrating no less than seven books.

An inventor and do-it-yourself hobbyist, Mr. Doty is the creator of the Popular Science Picture Clock Kit. He lives in Connecticut with his authoress wife and four children in one of the world's few solar-heated homes, which he helped design himself.

He has been twice voted Illustrator of the Year by the National Cartoonist Society and is the recipient of three Art Director Awards.

CAMEL DRIVERS ARE OVER THE HUMP

DRACULA WAS BATTY

HEIDI HAS A
SWISS BANK ACCOUNT

OLIVER
IS A
LITTLE DICKENS

MAID MARION MARRIED A HOOD

KING ARTHUR
RUNS A
KNIGHT SCHOOL

OLD KING COLE
HAD SOUL

COWBOYS HAVE CHAPPED KNEES

THE ST. LAWRENCE RIVER
IS HEADED FOR A FALL

MADAME BUTTERFLY WAS
ONCE A CATERPILLAR

MAGIC CARPETS HAVE TURBAN ENGINES

JOAN OF ARC WAS A FRENCH FRY

TAXIDERMISTS ARE STUFFY PEOPLE

PETER PAN WAS A FLY BY NIGHT

STAPLES GET IT ALL TOGETHER

DRACULA EATS AND RUNS

CENTAURS LIKE TO HORSE AROUND

ITTLE BO PEEP RUNS AROUND WITH A CROOK

THE RIO GRANDE TAKES IN BORDERS